Kids and Their Animal Friends

Table of Content

Table of Content

The Adventures of Max and His Best Friend

Part 1: Meet Max

Max was a happy and curious little boy who loved to explore the outdoors. One day, he was out on a walk in the woods when he stumbled upon a small, injured squirrel.

Part 2: Saving the Squirrel

Max carefully picked up the squirrel and brought it home, where he bandaged its wounds and gave it some food and water. The squirrel quickly recovered, and Max was overjoyed.

Part 3: The Friendship

Max and the squirrel quickly became friends, and Max named him Squeaky. Squeaky loved spending time with Max, and the two would go on all sorts of adventures together.

Part 4: A New Discovery

One day, Max and Squeaky were exploring a nearby creek when they saw a baby deer who had been separated from its mother. Max knew he had to help, so he carefully carried the baby deer back to its mother.

Part 5: A Mischievous Friend

As Max and Squeaky explored the woods, they came across a mischievous raccoon who loved to play pranks. Max and Squeaky quickly learned to keep an eye out for the raccoon's tricks.

Part 6: A Frightening Encounter

One day, Max and Squeaky were exploring a cave when they heard a loud growl. They quickly realized they had stumbled upon a mother bear and her cubs. Max knew they had to be very careful, so he slowly backed out of the cave and kept Squeaky close to him.

Part 7: A Helping Hand

Max and Squeaky often encountered animals in need, and they were always there to lend a helping hand. They helped lost birds find their way home and rescued animals who were trapped in traps.

Part 8: A Scary Storm

One stormy night, Max and Squeaky were at home when the power went out. Max was frightened, but Squeaky cuddled up next to him and kept him company until the power came back on.

Part 9: A Sad Goodbye

As the years went by, Max grew older, and Squeaky grew slower. One day, Squeaky passed away, leaving Max heartbroken. But he knew that Squeaky would always hold a special place in his heart.

Part 10: A Lifetime of Memories

Max never forgot about his adventures with Squeaky, and he often shared his stories with his own children and grandchildren. He knew that his animal friend had taught him valuable lessons about kindness, compassion, and the importance of friendship.

Part 9: A Sad Goodbye

As the years went by, Max grew older, and Squeaky grew slower. One day, Squeaky passed away, leaving Max heartbroken. But he knew that Squeaky would always hold a special place in his heart.

Part 10: A Lifetime of Memories

Max never forgot about his adventures with Squeaky, and he often shared his stories with his own children and grandchildren. He knew that his animal friend had taught him valuable lessons about kindness, compassion, and the importance of friendship.

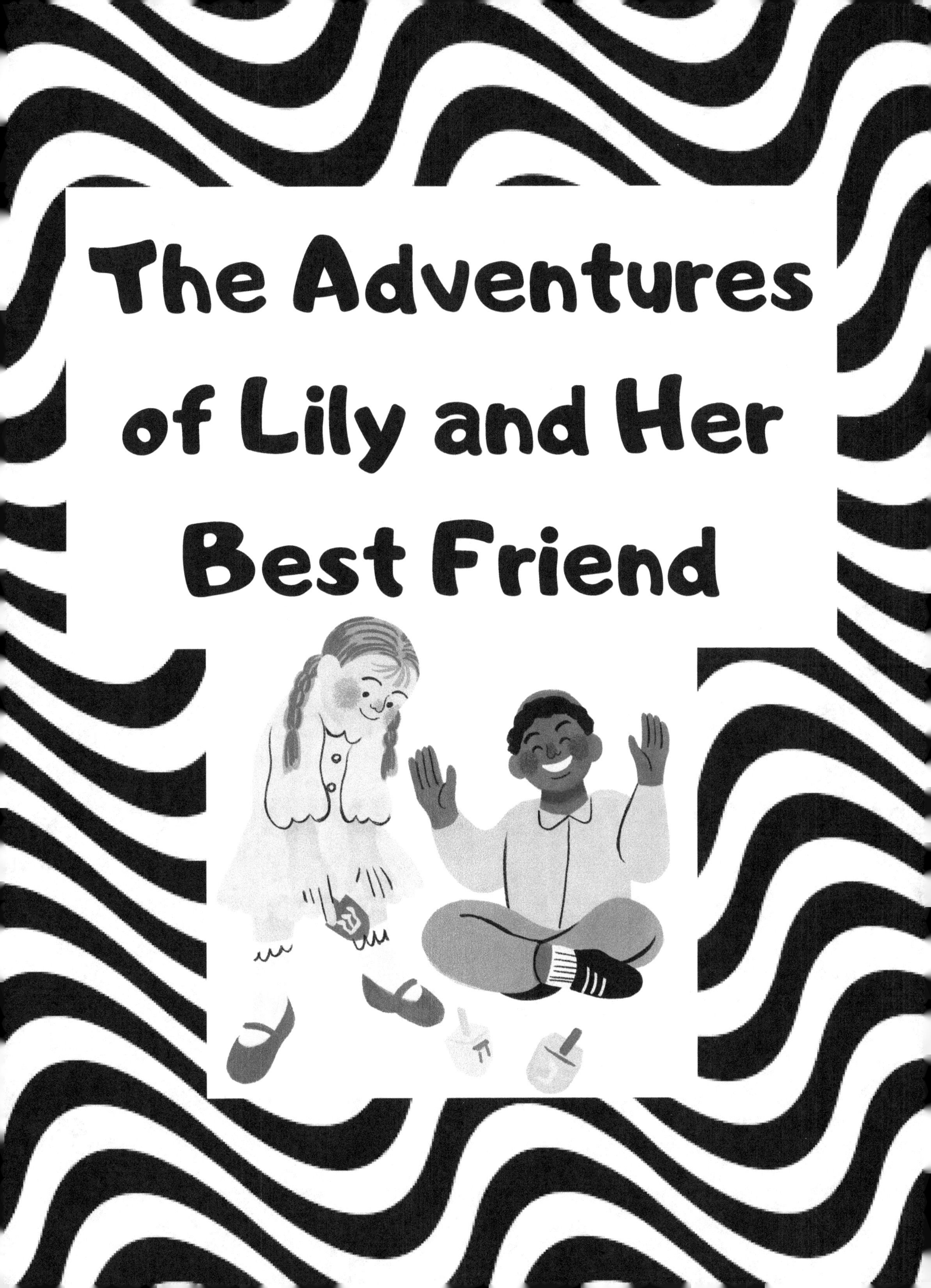

The Adventures of Lily and Her Best Friend

Part 1: Meet Lily

Lily was a sweet and curious little girl who loved spending time outdoors. One day, she was playing in the park when she stumbled upon a small, lost puppy.

Part 2: Rescuing the Puppy

Lily knew she had to help the puppy, so she took him home and gave him food, water, and a warm bed to sleep in. The puppy quickly became her best friend, and Lily named him Buddy.

Part 3: A Bond of Friendship

Lily and Buddy spent all their time together, exploring the woods and playing in the park. Buddy loved to run and fetch, and Lily loved to watch him play.

Part 4: An Unlikely Encounter

One day, Lily and Buddy were out on a walk when they saw a small, injured bird lying on the ground. Lily knew she had to help, so she carefully picked up the bird and brought it home.

Part 5: Healing the Bird

Lily and Buddy nursed the bird back to health, and soon it was strong enough to fly away. Lily felt proud of the help she had given, and Buddy wagged his tail in agreement.

Part 6: A New Friend

As Lily and Buddy explored the woods, they met a playful fox who loved to chase butterflies. Lily and Buddy quickly became friends with the fox, and the three of them would often play together.

Part 7: A Scary Situation

One day, Lily and Buddy were exploring a nearby creek when they heard a loud growl. They turned around to see a large, angry bear charging towards them. Lily quickly grabbed Buddy and ran as fast as she could.

Part 8: A Heartwarming Reunion

After the bear scare, Lily and Buddy were glad to be safe at home. But they soon received a heartwarming surprise when the lost puppy's owner came to claim him. Although they were sad to say goodbye, they were happy to see the puppy reunited with his family.

Part 9: A Lesson in Love

Lily knew that her time with Buddy was limited, as he was getting older and slower. But she loved him just the same, and cherished every moment they had together. She learned that love knows no bounds, and that the bond between a child and their animal friend is a special one.

Part 10: A Lifetime of Memories

Years went by, and Lily grew up to be a kind and compassionate adult. But she never forgot the adventures she shared with Buddy and the lessons he taught her about friendship, courage, and kindness. She often visited his grave, knowing that he would always hold a special place in her heart.

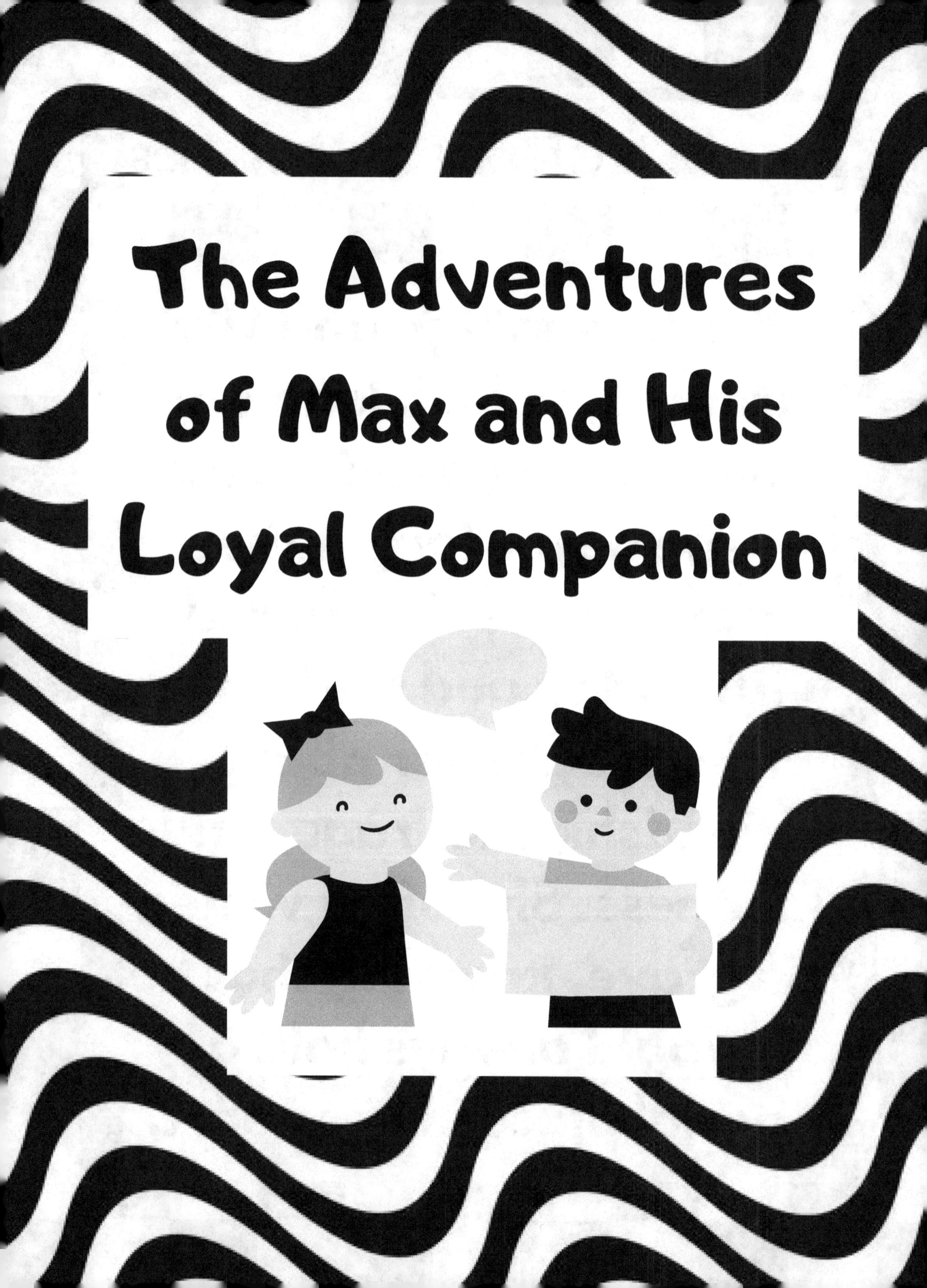
The Adventures
of Max and His
Loyal Companion

Part 1: The Meeting

Max was a young boy who loved spending his days exploring the great outdoors. One day, while he was wandering through the forest, he stumbled upon a small, injured wolf pup. Max knew he had to help the pup, so he brought him home and nursed him back to health.

Part 2: The Bond

As the pup grew stronger, Max and the wolf developed a deep bond. They spent their days exploring the forest together and going on exciting adventures. Max named the wolf his loyal companion and they became inseparable.

Part 3: The Discovery

One day, Max and his companion stumbled upon a hidden cave deep in the heart of the forest. They cautiously approached the entrance and peered inside, wondering what secrets lay within.

Part 4: The Treasure

As they entered the cave, Max and his companion discovered a hidden treasure trove of gold and jewels. But they quickly realized that the treasure belonged to a fierce dragon who had been guarding it for centuries.

Part 5: The Dragon

Max and his companion knew they had to be careful not to awaken the dragon. But as they were admiring the treasure, they accidentally made a noise that woke the dragon from its slumber.

Part 6: The Escape

Max and his companion raced out of the cave as fast as they could, with the dragon hot on their heels. They narrowly escaped the dragon's fiery breath and vowed never to return to the cave again.

Part 7: The Journey Home

As they made their way back home, Max and his companion talked about all the exciting adventures they had shared together. They knew that their bond was unbreakable and that they would always be there for each other, no matter what.

Part 8: The Return

Days turned into weeks, and weeks turned into months. Max and his companion continued to explore the forest and have amazing adventures together. But they knew that they had to return the treasure to the dragon, as it rightfully belonged to him.

Part 9: The Reconciliation

Max and his companion bravely returned to the dragon's cave and presented him with the treasure. The dragon was impressed by their bravery and loyalty, and he forgave them for taking the treasure in the first place.

Part 10: The Legacy

Max and his companion returned home, proud of the lessons they had learned and the bond they had formed. They knew that their friendship would last a lifetime and that they would continue to have many more adventures together, creating a legacy that would be remembered for generations to come.

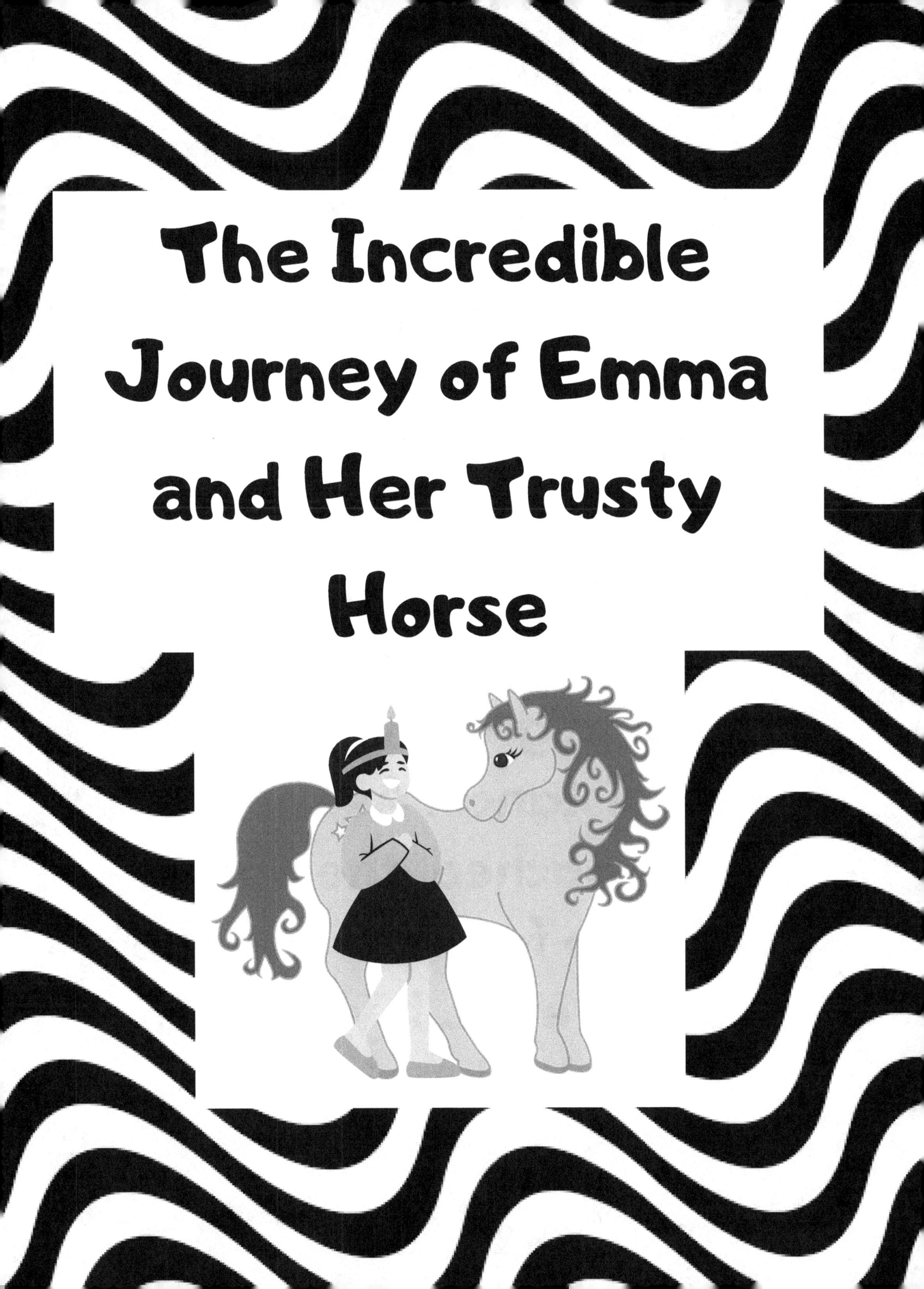

The Incredible Journey of Emma and Her Trusty Horse

Part 1: The Meeting

Emma was a young girl who loved animals and spent most of her days on her family's farm. One day, she was out in the fields when she saw a beautiful horse grazing in the distance. As she approached, the horse turned to face her and they locked eyes. It was as if they had an instant connection.

Part 2: The Bond

Emma knew she had to have the horse as her own, so she begged her parents to let her take care of him. They reluctantly agreed, and Emma and the horse developed a strong bond. She named him Thunder and he became her trusty companion.

Part 3: The Adventure

One day, Emma and Thunder set out on an adventure to explore the nearby forest. They rode for hours, enjoying the fresh air and the beautiful scenery. But as they ventured deeper into the woods, they got lost and couldn't find their way back.

Part 4: The Danger

As night fell, Emma and Thunder realized they were being watched by a pack of wolves. They knew they had to get away before the wolves attacked, so they raced off into the night.

Part 5: The Escape

Emma and Thunder rode as fast as they could, with the wolves hot on their heels. But just when it seemed like they would be caught, Thunder suddenly bolted down a narrow path that the wolves couldn't follow.

Part 6: The Encounter

As they continued on their journey, Emma and Thunder stumbled upon a group of travelers who were lost and in need of help. Emma knew she had to help them, so she led them to safety.

Part 7: The Reunion

Days turned into weeks, and Emma and Thunder continued their journey, never knowing what adventure would come next. But they knew they had to find their way back home, where their family was waiting for them.

Part 8: The Challenge

As they got closer to home, Emma and Thunder faced their biggest challenge yet. A raging river stood between them and their farm, and there was no way to cross it.

Part 9: The Solution

But Emma was determined to find a way across. She and Thunder searched for hours, until they found a fallen log that spanned the river. With Thunder's help, Emma was able to walk across the log and reach the other side.

Part 10: The Homecoming

Emma and Thunder finally made it back home, tired but victorious. They were welcomed with open arms by their family, who had been worried sick about them. Emma knew that she and Thunder had formed an unbreakable bond and that they would continue to have amazing adventures together for years to come.

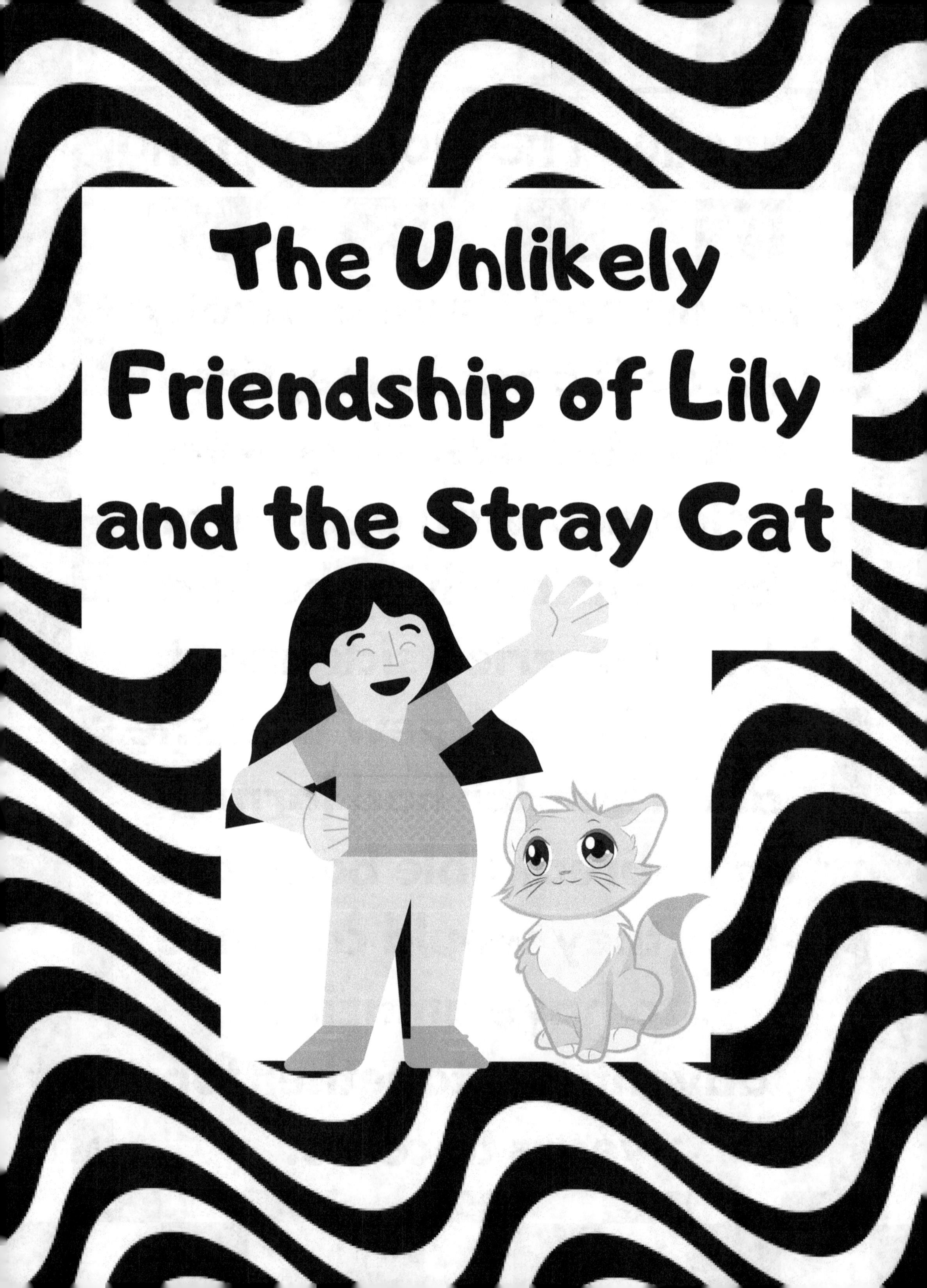

The Unlikely Friendship of Lily and the Stray Cat

Part 1: The Discovery

Lily was walking home from school one day when she spotted a small stray cat hiding in a bush. The cat looked frightened and alone, and Lily felt an immediate connection to it.

Part 2: The Rescue

Lily knew she had to help the cat, so she gently approached it and coaxed it out of the bush. The cat was wary at first, but soon began to trust Lily and allowed her to pick it up and carry it home.

Part 3: The Introduction

Lily's parents were hesitant about keeping a stray cat, but Lily was determined to take care of it. She named the cat Smudge and introduced it to her other pets, a dog named Max and a hamster named Peanut.

Part 4: The Friendship

To everyone's surprise, Smudge and Max became fast friends. They would play together for hours, chasing each other around the yard and cuddling up for naps.

Part 5: The Challenge

But one day, Smudge disappeared. Lily was devastated and searched high and low for her feline friend. Finally, she found Smudge hiding in a nearby alleyway, injured and unable to move.

Part 6: The Recovery

Lily immediately took Smudge to the vet, where they discovered that she had been hit by a car. Lily was determined to nurse Smudge back to health and spent hours each day caring for her.

Part 6: The Recovery

Lily immediately took Smudge to the vet, where they discovered that she had been hit by a car. Lily was determined to nurse Smudge back to health and spent hours each day caring for her.

Part 8: The Struggle

But the joy was short-lived, as Lily's family was facing financial struggles and could no longer afford to keep all of their pets. Lily was heartbroken at the thought of giving up Smudge.

Part 9: The Solution

Determined to keep Smudge, Lily came up with a plan. She started a fundraiser to raise money for Smudge's care and was amazed by the outpouring of support from her community.

Part 10: The Happy Ending

Thanks to Lily's hard work and the generosity of others, Smudge was able to stay with Lily and her family. Lily knew that she and Smudge had formed an unbreakable bond and that they would always be there for each other, no matter what challenges they may face in the future.

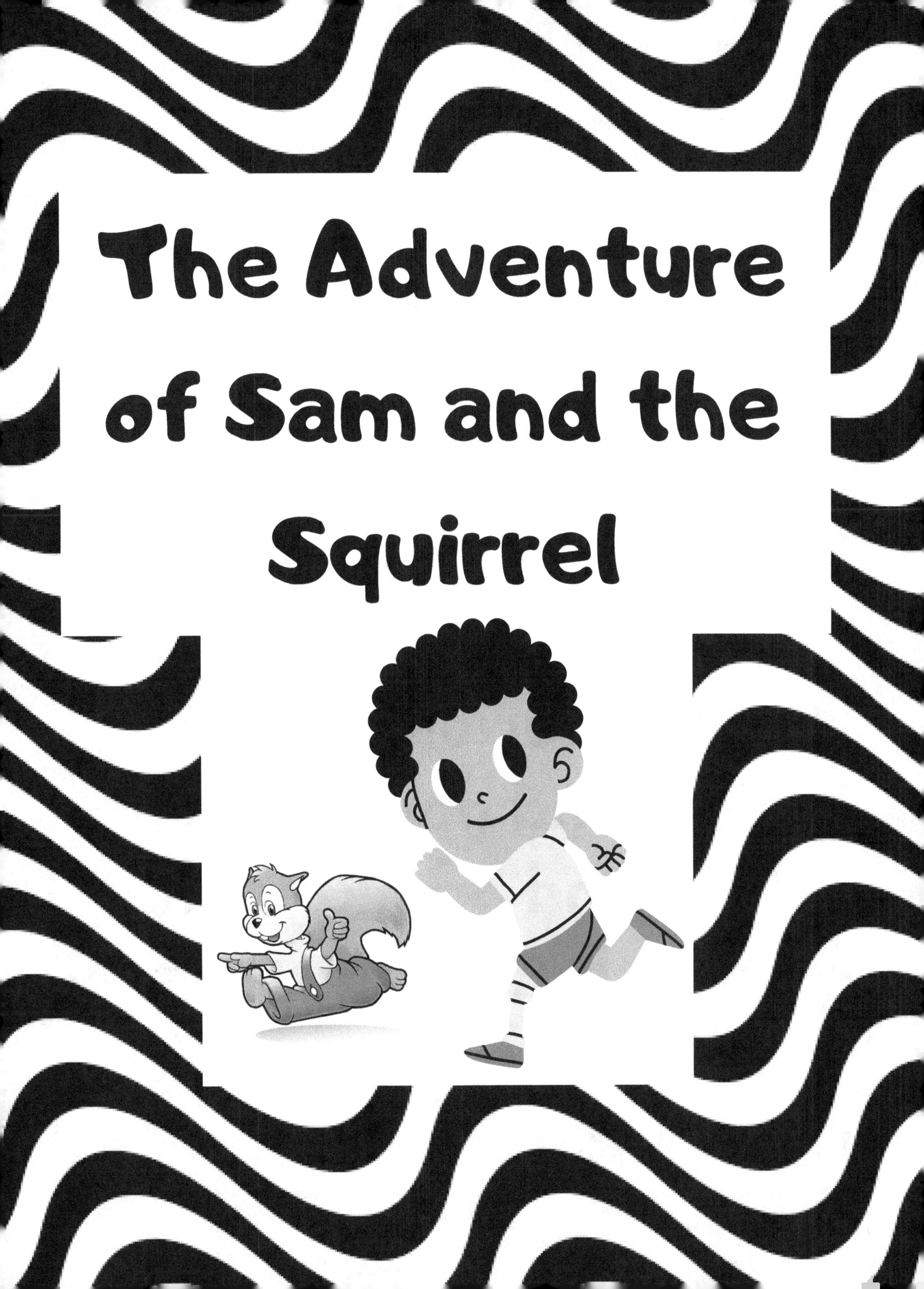

The Adventure of Sam and the Squirrel

Part 1: The Encounter

Sam was out exploring in the woods when he came across a small squirrel. The squirrel was curious about Sam and approached him, and Sam couldn't help but feel a sense of wonder about this little creature.

Part 2: The Bond

As Sam spent more time with the squirrel, he realized that they had formed a deep bond. The squirrel would follow him wherever he went, and even let Sam pet him and hold him in his hands.

Part 2: The Bond

As Sam spent more time with the squirrel, he realized that they had formed a deep bond. The squirrel would follow him wherever he went, and even let Sam pet him and hold him in his hands.

Part 2: The Bond

As Sam spent more time with the squirrel, he realized that they had formed a deep bond. The squirrel would follow him wherever he went, and even let Sam pet him and hold him in his hands.

Part 5: The Help

Sam knew he had to help the squirrel and his family, so he started leaving out food and water for them. The squirrel was grateful for Sam's help and soon started bringing his babies to meet him.

Part 6: The Obstacle

But soon, the squirrel family faced a new obstacle. A group of birds had taken over their tree and were threatening to kick them out.

Part 7: The Plan

Sam knew he had to come up with a plan to help his friends. He enlisted the help of his dog, who scared away the birds and helped the squirrel family reclaim their home.

Part 8: The Celebration

The squirrel family was overjoyed at being able to stay in their home, and Sam was thrilled to see them happy. He threw a small celebration for them, complete with nuts and berries.

Part 9: The Goodbye

As summer turned to fall, the squirrel family started preparing for winter. Sam knew that it was time to say goodbye, but he was comforted knowing that he had helped them and made a lasting impact on their lives.

Part 10: The Memory

Sam never forgot his adventure with the squirrel, and often thought about his little friend and the joy they had brought to each other's lives. He knew that their friendship was something special and that it would always hold a special place in his heart.

The Friendship of Lily and the Fawn

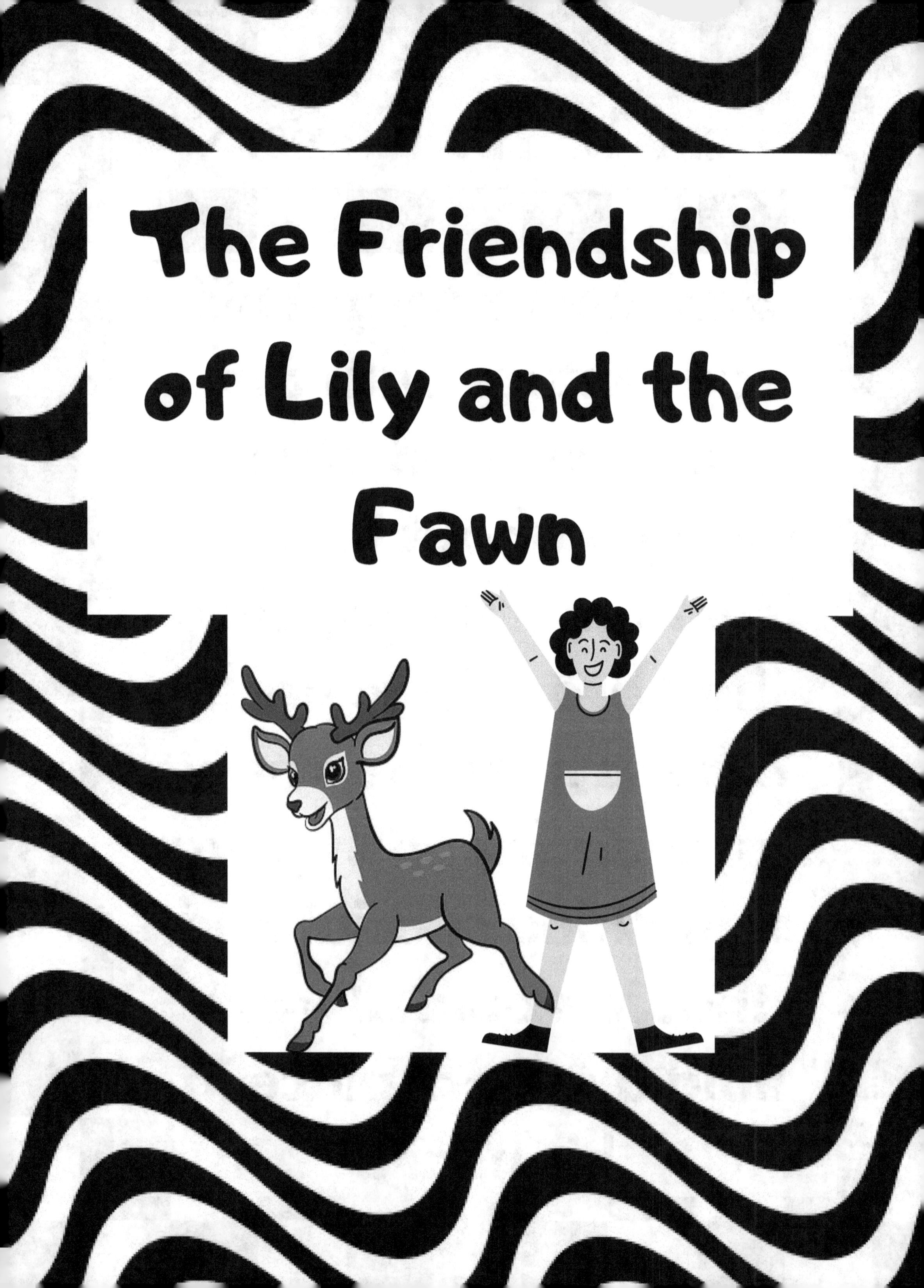

Part 1: The Discovery

Lily was walking through the forest when she came across a fawn. The little animal was lying in a clearing, and Lily was immediately drawn to its delicate features.

Part 2: The Rescue

Lily soon realized that the fawn was injured, with a deep cut on its leg. She knew she had to help, so she gently picked the fawn up and took it back to her home.

Part 3: The Bond

As Lily nursed the fawn back to health, they formed a deep bond. The fawn would follow her around the house, and even snuggled up with her on the couch.

Part 4: The Surprise

But one day, the fawn's mother came looking for her baby. Lily was surprised to see the mother deer standing in her yard, but knew she had to return the fawn to its rightful place.

Part 5: The Reunion

Lily brought the fawn back to the clearing where she had found it, and was happy to see it reunited with its mother. The two deer ran off into the forest together, leaving Lily feeling both happy and sad.

Part 6: The Return

Days later, the fawn returned to Lily's yard, with its mother following close behind. Lily was thrilled to see her little friend again, and knew that their friendship was something special.

Part 7: The Secret

Lily knew that it was important to keep the fawn's visits a secret, so she only told her closest friends about her animal friend. They were amazed by her story and promised to keep it to themselves.

Part 8: The Adventure

Lily and the fawn had many adventures together, exploring the forest and playing in the fields. They even made a secret hideout in the woods, where they could spend time together away from prying eyes.

Part 9: The Farewell

As the seasons changed and the fawn grew stronger, Lily knew that it was time to say goodbye. She knew that the fawn needed to be with its family in the wild, but it was hard to let go of her animal friend.

Part 10: The Memory

Lily never forgot her friendship with the fawn, and often thought about their adventures together. She knew that their bond was something special, and that their friendship would always hold a special place in her heart.

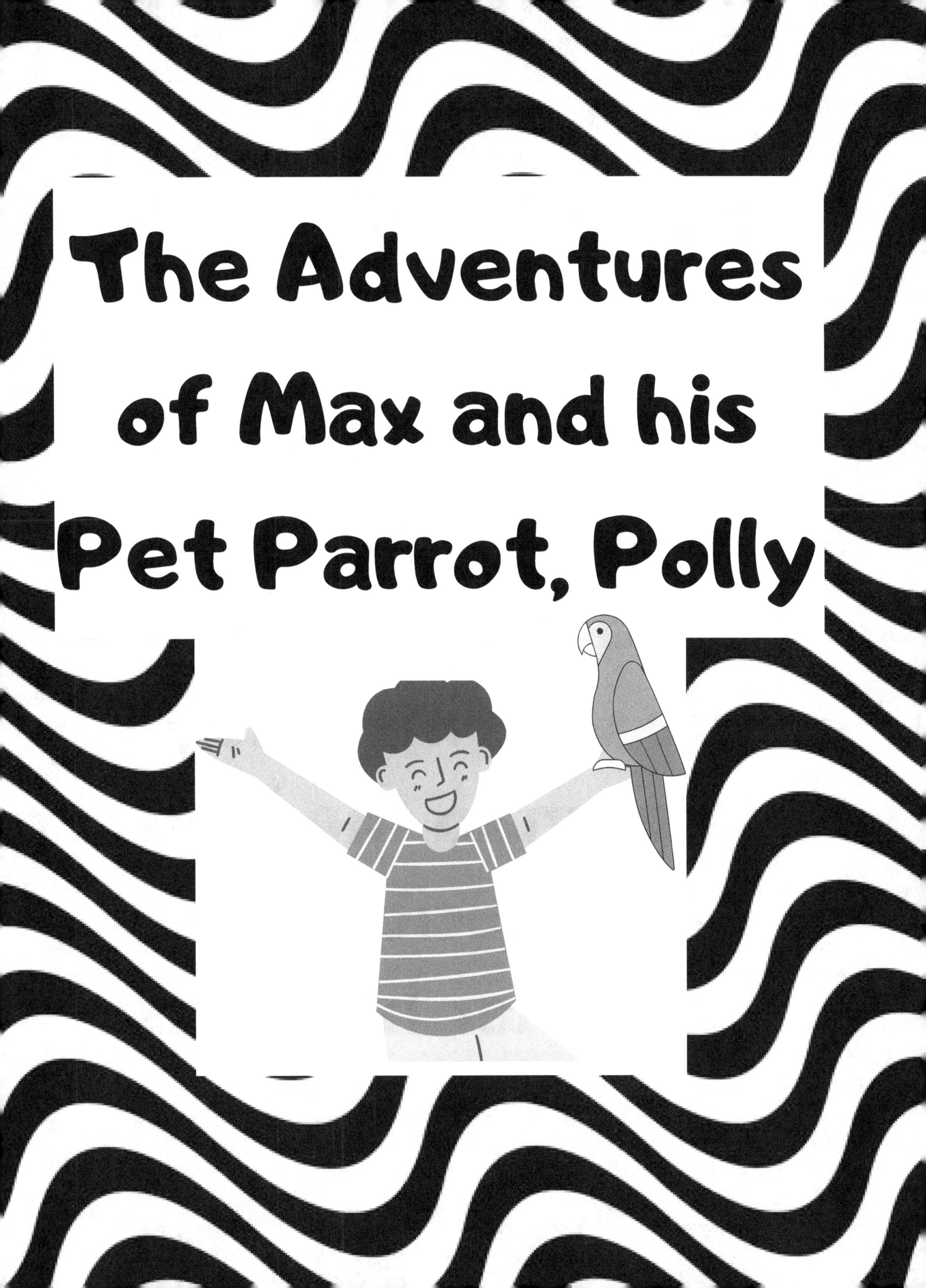

The Adventures
of Max and his
Pet Parrot, Polly

Part 1: The Pet Store

Max was visiting the pet store when he saw a colorful parrot named Polly. He was instantly drawn to the bird and decided to bring her home as his new pet.

Max and Polly didn't hit it off at first. The bird was feisty and didn't like being held, but Max was determined to win her over.

Part 3: The Training

Max spent hours training Polly, teaching her tricks and playing games. Eventually, the parrot warmed up to him and became his loyal companion.

Part 4: The Secret

Max soon discovered that Polly was a clever bird, and could even mimic human speech. He taught her to keep their conversations a secret, so no one else would know that she could talk.

Part 5: The Escape

One day, Max left Polly's cage open by mistake, and the bird flew out into the yard. Max was worried that she would fly away for good, but Polly came back to him, landing on his shoulder.

Part 6: The Adventure

Max and Polly went on many adventures together, exploring the neighborhood and even visiting the park. Polly would sit on Max's shoulder and watch the world go by, occasionally letting out a squawk or two.

Part 7: The Rescue

One day, Max and Polly stumbled upon a baby bird that had fallen out of its nest. Max knew he had to help, so he carefully picked up the bird and brought it home to care for it.

Part 8: The Growing Family

Max and Polly became the proud owners of two birds, with the new baby bird growing stronger every day. Polly became a surrogate mother to the baby bird, and the three birds became a happy family.

Part 9: The Secret's Out

One day, Max's best friend came over to play and overheard Polly talking. Max was worried that the secret was out, but his friend promised to keep it to himself.

Part 10: The Goodbye

Years later, Max had to say goodbye to Polly, who had grown old and passed away. He was sad to lose his beloved pet, but knew that their adventures together would live on in his memories forever.

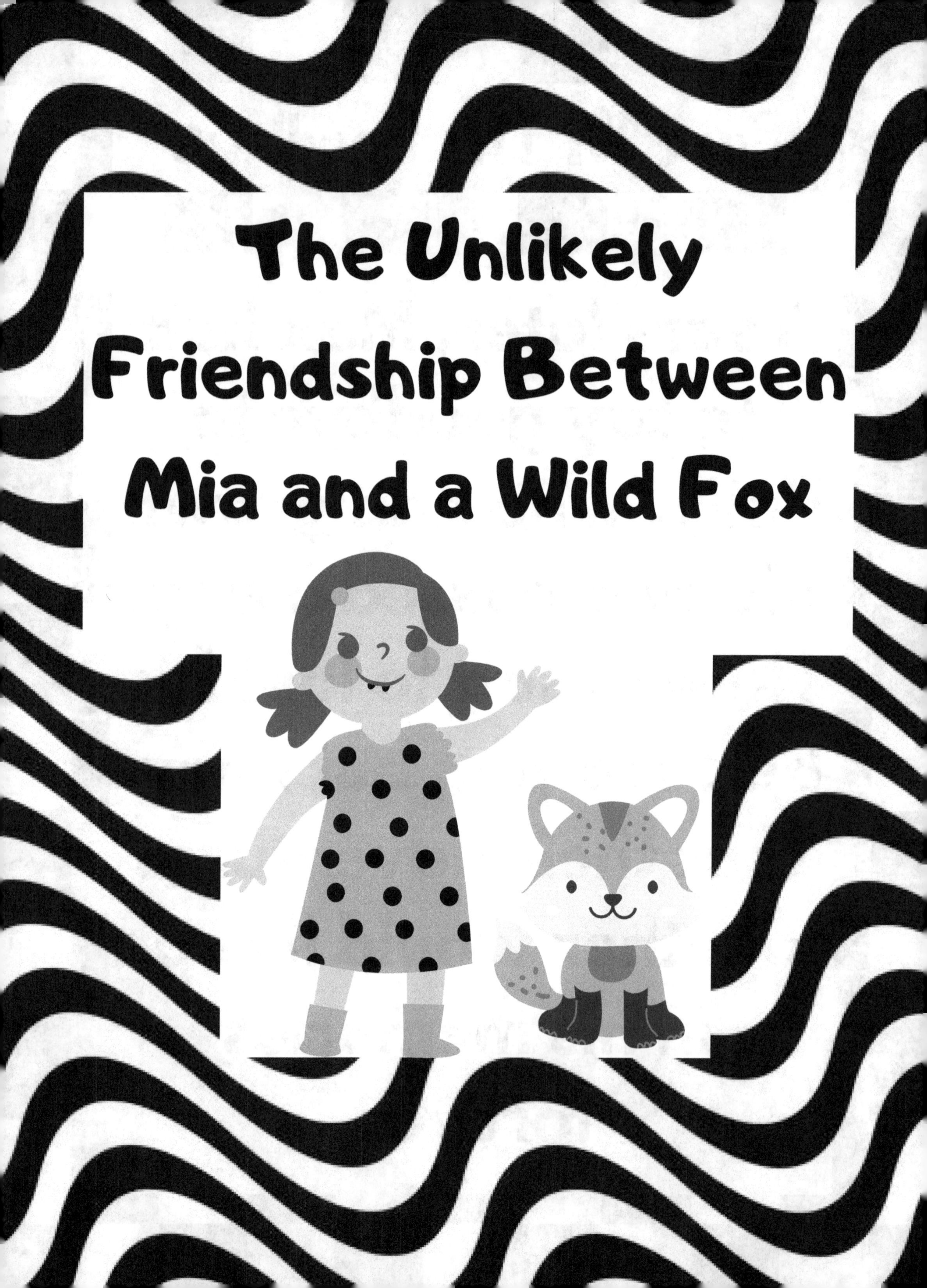

The Unlikely Friendship Between Mia and a Wild Fox

Part 1: The Encounter

Mia was walking through the forest near her home when she stumbled upon a small fox that was injured and unable to move. She felt sorry for the animal and decided to help it.

Part 2: The Healing

Mia took the fox back to her house and tended to its wounds. She nursed it back to health and slowly gained its trust.

Part 3: The Friendship

As the fox healed, it and Mia developed an unlikely friendship. They would play together in the backyard and go on adventures in the nearby woods.

Part 4: The Secret

Mia kept the fox a secret from her parents, knowing that they would not approve of her bringing a wild animal into their home.

Part 5: The Betrayal

One day, a neighbor saw Mia playing with the fox and reported it to the authorities. Animal control came and took the fox away, leaving Mia heartbroken.

Part 6: The Reunion

After weeks of searching and making phone calls, Mia was finally able to locate the fox in a wildlife rehabilitation center. She visited the fox every day, determined to bring it back home with her.

Part 7: The Plan

Mia devised a plan to rescue the fox from the center. She recruited some of her friends to help distract the guards while she snuck in and grabbed the fox.

Part 8: The Escape

The plan worked, and Mia was able to escape with the fox. She took it back home, where it lived with her in secret once again.

Part 9: The Goodbye

As the fox grew older, it became increasingly difficult for Mia to keep it hidden. Eventually, she knew that she would have to let it go back into the wild.

Part 10: The Legacy

Mia released the fox back into the forest where she first found it. She knew that it would be difficult to say goodbye, but she also knew that she had formed a lifelong bond with the animal, and that it would never forget the kindness that Mia had shown it.